Practical

WATER GARDENING

Yvonne Rees

The Crowood Press

First published in 1994 by
The Crowood Press Ltd
Ramsbury, Marlborough
Wiltshire SN8 2HR

British Library Cataloguing-in-Publication Data

A catalogue record for this book is available from the British
Library.

ISBN 1 85223 623 X

Picture Credits
Photographs on pages 19, 20, 25, 26, 30, 38 (left), 40, 42, 43,
45, 47, 49, 52 and 56 by Yvonne Rees; page 31 (left), by Dave
Pike; page 37 (left), courtesy of Lotus Water Gardens; and
pages 49 (top) and 51, courtesy of Hozelock. All remaining
photographs by Sue Atkinson.

Typeset in Optima by Chippendale Type Ltd,
Otley, West Yorkshire
Printed and bound by Paramount Printing Group, Hong Kong

CONTENTS

INTRODUCTION

There is simply no excuse for not having a water feature in your garden. It can be designed to suit any site: large or small. There is something to meet any budget, any style – there are even safe options for families who have young children. The benefits are immeasurable: for a little outlay of time and cash (and maybe your investment will be as modest as an old barrel and a couple of goldfish) you acquire a delightful garden feature – perhaps even a stunning one – that will give you many hours of pleasure for minimum maintenance. A pond, a fountain or even a simple water spout is an instant focal point. The kind of plants that grow in and around water are bold and dramatic: exotic looking water lilies, spiky rushes and plants like *Rheum palmatum* with huge leaves as big as 5ft (1.5m) across. They are fun to grow and exciting to see.

An impressive display of foliage shapes and colours from the inverted umbrellas of outsize Gunnera *to feathery green ferns and the dense quilted leaves of a blue-hued hosta.*

A space-saving pool in a corner of the patio features a wall-mounted lion's head fed by a submersible pump in the pool.

Water adds something special to your scheme too: the mirror gleam of water adding light and space; the sense of movement with sky and clouds caught in the water's surface, or the sparkle and shimmer of a moving water feature. There are also gentle sounds: the ripple and *splip* of a fishpool, the tinkle of a fountain or rush of stream and waterfall. All these sights and sounds distract from the tensions of everyday life and mask the hurly-burly babble of life beyond the garden, so a water feature is very relaxing. No wonder they are so popular in town gardens as an antidote to stress; or that the Japanese make them an essential element of their tranquil courtyard and garden schemes.

A pond, particularly, has an additional advantage: it acts like a magnet for wildlife. Even if you do not stock it yourself with fish, snails and frogs, a remarkable variety of animals will appear as if by magic even in the most urban setting. They will not have all hopped, wriggled or walked their way to your garden: eggs are often brought on the bills of visiting birds and many of the aquatic creatures arrive courtesy of your pond plants. You can expect to see water boatmen skimming the surface, glossy beetles, frogs, toads, perhaps newts, beautiful dragonflies and bees and butterflies too,

Pretty primulas are set against a dramatic watery backdrop with this vertical cascade.

Water playing over a millstone into a bowl of pebbles makes an attractive feature for a corner of the courtyard, conservatory or patio.

attracted by lush-growing water plants. You will find a greater variety of birds visiting the garden, as well as small mammals looking for a drink. An even greater variety of wildlife can be expected if you plan your pond specifically for that purpose, with a

sloping shallow end which enables creatures to get down to the water more easily and a 'green passageway' of trees and shrubs linking the pool to their nearby natural habitat.

Water features have been with us since gardens for pleasure first began: natural lakes and pools were an integral part of the Zen-inspired garden landscapes of ancient China and Japan; while formal pools and fountains were commonly seen in the inner

A series of small cascades into a formal pool makes a delightful feature for garden or patio.

courtyards of the earliest homes in the Middle and Far East where they had a welcome cooling effect in a hot climate. Some of the most famous gardens of the world have been based around water – look at the Moor-inspired Alhambra with its fountains and canals, and Louis XIV's remarkable gardens at Versailles outside Paris which in their heyday used a remarkable system of watermills and pumps to take water from the Seine to run 1,400 fountains.

By the eighteenth century, the fashion was for a natural landscape rather than an elaborate arrangement of formal pools, fountains and water novelties. The Romantic landscape garden movement in England excavated lakes, dammed valleys and built false hills, with English landscaping's most famous son Lancelot (Capability) Brown creating such classic water features as the Great Water Staircase at Chatsworth in Derbyshire.

Today we are accustomed to water as a familiar part of the architectural landscape, as well as in parks and gardens. Many a new office building incorporates a pool or water sculpture at the entrance; where this is not possible then perhaps there is a fountain or fish-pool in the foyer.

Water is a wonderful antidote to a stressful life-style and where better to enjoy it at your leisure than in the peace and privacy of your own yard? It's very versatility easily makes the dream a reality.

1 • CHOOSING A WATER FEATURE

Once you have decided you would like a water feature – maybe a pond or self-contained bubble fountain – you should think the project through carefully before you rush out and start work on construction. It is worth considering from the start whether you could be a little more ambitious with your plans. While you are going to the trouble of installing a water feature, perhaps it could be bigger, more exciting or better suited to your garden or patio plan. Water is wonderfully flexible and there really is no limit to the number of ways it can be incorporated into a design. For inspiration, browse through gardening magazines and books, visit a specialist water garden centre or the water garden section of your local garden centre. Most have a selection of features constructed that you can view and walk around. Many gardens open to the public also include some form of lake, pool or formal water feature if you are looking for good ideas – and you can always scale them down or adapt a theme if your little patch is not quite in the same league. Jot down the ideas which most appeal to you, then consider how practical they might be in your own garden.

You will need to be completely familiar with your existing back yard or garden layout. Drawing up a scaled plan is a great help to see the overview more clearly. You can plot in existing permanent features such as the patio, any garden buildings, trees and so on, and indicate any changes of level and also which areas are sunny or shady. Looking at the scheme as a whole, the best size and shape feature should suggest itself. It may be worth altering part of your existing layout to accommodate a particularly good idea. Naturally the final scheme should be harmonious, the water fully integrated with other features – either to create a focal point, or as part of a larger plan. A pool might continue the line of a curve for example, or form part of a series of interlocking geometric shapes. The thing to avoid is for

Another point of interest within your garden plan, such as a summer-house or gazebo, may suggest a suitable setting for your water feature.

your water feature to stand alone, like a kind of island, with no bearing on its surroundings.

Apart from any restrictions created by the size and shape of the site, or the presence of existing features, the site of a pool is subject to other, very practical limitations. Pools do not need perfect conditions by any means, but the position must receive plenty of light if you want to grow moisture-loving plants. This is necessary so that the sunlight can penetrate the water and allow aquatic plants to photosynthesize and maintain the dissolved oxygen level in the water. You might be advised that too much sunlight creates a problem with 'green water' – excessive green algae growth – but this is more due to the fact that there are too many nutrients and not enough predators, an ecological imbalance that can be corrected in a variety of ways (*see* page 54).

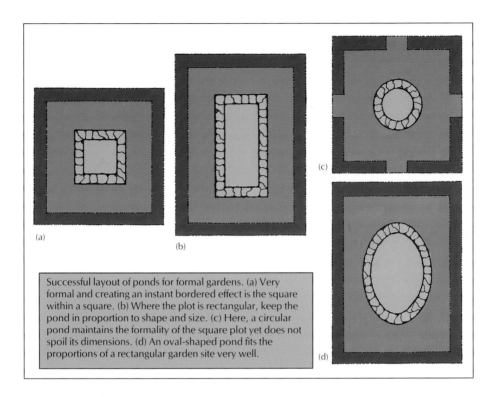

Successful layout of ponds for formal gardens. (a) Very formal and creating an instant bordered effect is the square within a square. (b) Where the plot is rectangular, keep the pond in proportion to shape and size. (c) Here, a circular pond maintains the formality of the square plot yet does not spoil its dimensions. (d) An oval-shaped pond fits the proportions of a rectangular garden site very well.

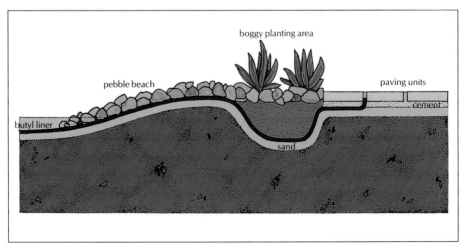

A sloping pebble beach enters a pool gradually and looks particularly attractive combined with a rock garden or oriental water garden.

A pool also needs protection from draughts or prevailing winds, as lush water plants will suffer from wind burn or broken stems. A wall or fence makes an efficient windbreak, provided it is only required to give protection to a distance of around three times its height away. This will ensure maximum sunlight while still receiving shelter. A broken windbreak such as a hedge, screen or trellis is better as this filters the wind and reduces it, rather than just deflecting it. Ideally, as you face your feature, the highest part of it should be furthest away from you and this should be towards the north; however, a south-facing site is not essential provided you keep it as southerly as possible. Where this is too difficult, an easterly aspect is preferable if you can provide shelter from winds.

Not a plant for small gardens, but a wonderfully dramatic focal-point where you have the space to grow it, giant *Gunnera manicata* produces a huge clump of round, prickly-edged leaves each up to 5ft (1.5m) across. It prefers a moist soil which is why you often see it beside a pond or pool, or as part of a bold bog garden planting scheme, and a sunny position. Although the plant is hardy, it does need protection from cold winds and an effective mulch for the crown in winter – some of the large leaves are usually folded over for this. Light green flower spikes appear in early summer to be followed by orange-brown seed pods.

A circular raised pool is not particularly simple to construct, but it makes a very attractive feature within a formal design, especially if you are planning to include a central fountain.

You will find the deeper the pool, the less likely it is to freeze solid, provided it is a sunken one. The soil holds the warmth, and a depth of at least 3ft (90cm) is recommended – but no deeper than 4ft (120cm) – if you intend to keep fish. Even this cannot guarantee that the water will not freeze solid under extreme conditions, and over-wintering indoors or using a pool heater is recommended (*see* page 54). A raised pool is far more exposed and highly likely to freeze with no protection. Incidentally, if you are planning to keep fish seriously, you will also have to consider how you will protect the pool from predators and how to keep the fish from jumping out – even quite small Koi can jump as high as 24in (60cm).

Your feature must also be away from any deciduous shrubs or trees which might create a nuisance with falling leaves in autumn. If you have young children or pets likely to be a problem with the water, you will have to plan a feature with an underground, hidden reservoir; or, if you have a pond or pool, it should be efficiently fenced.

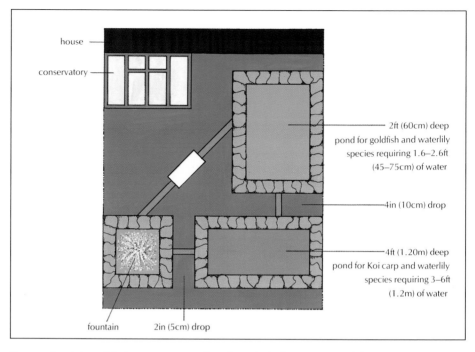

house

conservatory

2ft (60cm) deep pond for goldfish and waterlily species requiring 1.6–2.6ft (45–75cm) of water

4in (10cm) drop

4ft (1.20m) deep pond for Koi carp and waterlily species requiring 3–6ft (1.2m) of water

fountain   2in (5cm) drop

Your garden design might incorporate several pools, each displaying a range of different water features and including both deep and shallow water. The pools might be linked by a small cascade, a bridge, a path or by stepping-stones.

Size and Style

Size is not as much of a restriction as you might at first think. Even a small garden can be home to a large water feature. In fact, this bold treatment frequently pays off by making the garden seem bigger and certainly more interesting than it really is. It would often be better to develop a large pond or pool garden complete with a full range of bog and water plants, decked patio area and bridges or stepping-stones than to try and combine several features – small pool, paved patio, lawn, flower beds, for example – into a limited area. Going in the other direction, the smallest water feature has its attractions whether it be a lion's head attached to a wall and spouting water, a

barrel bog garden, or simply an attractive stone bowl of water. However, if you would like a traditional pool with a full range of plants and wildlife, it should be at least 6 × 4ft (180 × 120cm) and a minimum of 2ft (60cm) deep.

The style of your existing (or proposed) garden will determine whether you choose a formal water feature or a more naturalistic effect. Both can look superb in the right setting. Symmetry tends to be the controlling factor of the formal feature. Geometric shapes such as squares, rectangles, circles and ovals predominate; there are lots of straight lines and symmetrically-placed or interlocking features – a theme into which a pond or similar self-contained water features can fit very well. A pond, well defined

Always plan your water feature with the rest of the garden in mind so that you can set it in the right context.

by a sharp edging of brick or pavers, makes a fine centre-piece to a regularly-shaped plot, particularly if it echoes the shape of the whole. Alternatively, a circular free-standing fountain might be used as the central focal-point of a patio scheme. Where a central feature does not suit the plot, interlocking geometric shapes, often on different levels and incorporating fountains, cascades and water chutes, are particularly successful and give a garden or patio design a very professional look.

Since marginal plants create a rather unruly if dramatic outline, these are usually kept to a minimum in the formal water garden, perhaps even restricted to containers where they can be more easily controlled. Water-lilies are a different matter, their classic shape and wonderful blooms the perfect decoration for a formal pool.

Informal water features need planning with equal care and precision for, while they must never look contrived, that natural

A change of level within a patio pool design means the pools can be linked using a small cascade.

look is achieved only through careful attention to detail and proper construction. They do not come about by accident, even if they look that way. It helps to study ponds, streams and waterfalls in the wild before you start: see how they follow the contours of the land, the way the plants grow and the rocks lie. Adapt these principles to your own garden and you will be rewarded with a feature that looks perfectly in keeping with its surroundings.

This small cascade and sparsely planted formal pool are simply designed but essential to the overall theme of the garden providing a welcome change of life and texture.

Suiting a Theme

Water is so adaptable that there is a feature to suit every style of garden – and patio or courtyard too. Here water is useful, either as a moving water feature to add a sparkle of interest, or as a pool (or pools) to break up all that hard landscaping with a softer, more ethereal surface. For the classical garden there are elegant, not necessarily symmetrical, pools edged in old stone and featuring tasteful accessories such as

Astilbe is a useful pool edge or bog garden species, not just for its hardiness and tolerance of partial shade – in fact some varieties prefer it – but for its lovely feathery flower spikes which stand proud above the mass of foliage in shades of pink, red or white. It likes a rich moist soil and looks particularly good in large clumps bordering a pool or stream. Another big plus in *Astilbe*'s favour is that it is virtually maintenance free. The flowers look just as good in winter after they have turned brown, and they prefer to grow undisturbed. A mulch of well rotted manure in spring will encourage good growth. You can propagate new plants by seed in autumn or by division of established plants in spring or autumn.

arching fountains and statuary. This idea is sometimes developed into something rather different, indeed taken to its extreme, in the ornamental garden where plants take second place to accessories, ornaments and highly decorative paving and walling

An informal bog garden can be linked to a natural pond and used to grow a fascinating collection of moisture-loving plants.

It takes a year or two for hardy perennial *Rodgersia pinnata* to become established, but it is worth it for the large panicles of fluffy white, pink or red flowers which will appear in late spring and which can be more than 36in (90cm) tall. The foliage is equally dramatic, being deeply cut and veined. This is a plant that thrives in moist soil and does not like full sun, so is useful grown in the shade of a much larger plant at the water's edge. New plants can be propagated by seed in autumn or by division in spring. *R. p.* 'Superba' is particularly attractive with bright green, bronze-tinged leaves and star-shaped bright pink flowers in summer.

elements. Here a pool might feature a water-spouting figure, an ornate bridge or other water-related artefacts. Alternatively, a bubble fountain might be arranged foaming over some decorative object. If a rockery or alpine garden is dominant in your scheme, a rocky waterfall and pool are an obvious choice and a stunning landscape combination. Few garden features are so complementary.

A pool is also an essential element of the wildlife garden, an increasingly popular concept as much for city sites as rural ones, where they provide a valuable refuge and 'stepping-stone' for many wildlife species if thoughtfully planned. This is where an informal pool comes into its own, providing habitat and watering-hole for a wide variety of insects, small mammals and birds.

Water is also one of the vital elements of the oriental philosophy of gardening, where it might take the form of a large, natural pool or lake edged by mossy boulders and a shingle beach, or a small but exquisite traditional moving water feature among a raked sand and rock courtyard.

2 • BUILDING A POND

A pond can be virtually any size or shape, either raised or sunken, and will be lined to contain the water in one of four ways: puddled clay – the most natural way and often chosen for large pools; concrete which was how ponds were traditionally lined; a rubber or plastic liner which has largely replaced concrete; or a fibreglass mould.

Preparing the Site

The shape of your pool will have to be mapped out on the ground and checked from every angle to see if it looks as good in reality as it did on your plan. Formal shapes will require the use of a set-square and straight-edge to create the correct geometric figure. It helps to make a large-scale set-square for getting an accurate right angle. Three lengths of wood in the ratio 3:4:5 fastened together with nails or screws to form a triangle will guarantee a 90 degree

If you are not restricted to using a preformed liner, the shape and style of your pool are limited only by your imagination.

The Japanese butterburr or *Petasites japonicus* is a valuable large-leaved marginal plant with a creeping habit that makes it a dramatic and useful ground cover plant, if a rather invasive one. It is not particularly fussy concerning situation or soil provided the position is moist, so is often grown to cover difficult cool shady sites. Attractive yellow flowers appear in spring and their high nectar content makes this a good bee plant for the garden.

angle. Circular or oval shapes can be drawn using a centre peg and string. To describe an oval, you need two fixed stakes and a loop of string into which a peg is fixed to draw out the shape. The closer together your stakes, the more circular the final shape will be. Irregular shapes can be approximated with pegs and string or a length of hosepipe. A rough kidney or leg-of-mutton shape are the most popular, but try not to have too many indentations and inlets as they serve no practical purpose and make the pool difficult to construct.

When you are happy with its size and shape, a sunken pool will have to be excavated. Begin by stripping the turf away by cutting it into long strips with a sharp-edged spade, rolling these up root-side out and storing them in a damp place. These can be used later to edge your pool or be utilized elsewhere in the garden. The next stage is to remove the topsoil and place it carefully to one side where again it can be re-used, if not as part of your new feature then elsewhere. The subsoil must now be excavated to the required depth and used to landscape the surrounding area or be removed totally, depending on your plans. Ideal pool depth

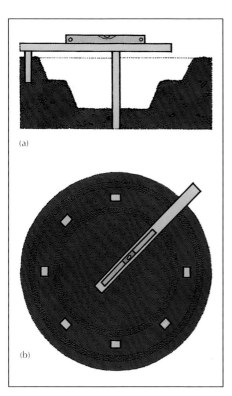

(a)

(b)

Yellow flag, *Iris pseudacorus*, is a common sight along the river-banks of Europe and Central Asia, streaking the countryside with swathes of bright green and yellow. It grows well in the water garden being hardy and a prolific grower, preferring semi-shade and a damp, marginal position. Flowers appear early to mid summer and the light green leaves are sword shaped, often with a kind of bluish tinge to them. There is a variegated version 'Variegata' which features attractive green and yellow striped foliage in spring which turns green before flowering.

Levelling a pool. (a) Levelling an informal pool: make a straight-edge using a length of warp-free wood that is long enough to run from a stake in the centre of the pool to a peg on the bank. Place a spirit-level on the wood to determine whether the pool is level. Check at every stage. (b) Levelling a circular pool: pivoting your straight-edge and spirit-level to different points around the pool's circumference will enable you to check whether a circular feature is level.

Excavation should incorporate a shelf about 10in (25cm) below the final level of the water and around 12in (30cm) wide. This is for positioning your marginal plants – that is, those that prefer to grow partly submerged in water. It is essential that the sides are level; drive a 4ft (1.2m) post in the centre and use a straight-edge between this point and one of your smaller 12in (30cm) perimeter pegs with a spirit-level along the top to check. Check and double check all the way round.

All but the smallest pools will require a mechanical digger. These can be hired by the day or weekend, so it is worth estimating exactly how long you think the job will take and making sure the site is ready. Various machines are available according to the size of hole you require. A small dumper-mounted back hoe will dig to a maximum depth of 5ft (1.5m) and is fairly easy to operate, but something like a Bob-cat

is between 2–4ft (60cm–1.2m) and it is a good idea to try and angle the sides at about 20 degrees. If you are lining the pool in concrete this makes the job a little easier and will also allow winter ice to rise up instead of expanding and inevitably damaging the sides.

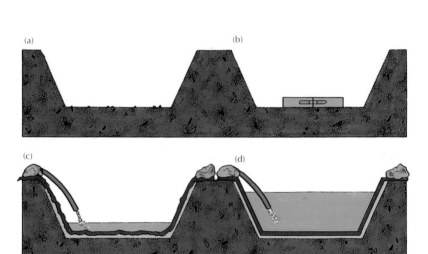

Stretching a rubber or PVC liner into place. (a) The pond is excavated to your chosen shape. (b) Use a spirit-level to check that it is all completely level. Make sure that there are no sharp stones. (c) Place the liner over the hole. Feed in sufficient liner to fit the cavity. Place rocks or boulders with no sharp edges around the edge to anchor it in place. (d) Allow the water to trickle in gently through a hosepipe. As the liner fills, ease it into position, making the necessary tucks and folds, and remove the anchor rocks from the edges to prevent the liner from tearing.

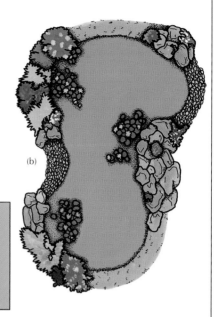

(a)

(b)

Types of pool. (a) Small ornamental pools about 32sq ft (3sq m) can be excavated by hand or light machinery. (b) A small natural pond should be excavated into an irregular shape about 26ft (8m) long. Plants and boulders help to soften the edges. A larger informal pond of, say, 43ft (12m) in length would have to be excavated mechanically and clay puddled.

is recommended for small and medium-sized pools since it has the advantage of being able to transport the excavated soil elsewhere (something else you must have decided before work starts – where the waste is all going to go) and you do not need a skilled operator. For larger pools and sloping sites, you will need a JCB and a trained operator to use it. However, it does an extremely quick and effective job. Large pools and difficult conditions are better off with a Hymac, which is usually hired by the hour and includes a skilled operator. This is used in conjunction with dumper trucks or skips to remove the soil. With all these machines you must ensure you have suitable access to the site. It may be necessary to crane the digger over a fence or wall and this will add to the cost. If the pond is small and you will be digging out by hand you will need a wood saw, posts and pegs, a

spade, shovel and pickaxe. A wheelbarrow with inflatable tyres is best for taking heavy loads across uneven ground.

When your pool has been excavated and you are sure it is level, check for and remove any stones or sharp objects, then smooth out any bumps or hollows. If you are using a concrete liner, finish with a binding layer of sand about ½in (13mm) thick. For plastic and rubber liners, old carpet, sacking or proprietary pool under-lining is necessary. Mould it to the shape as best you can.

Top-Ups and Overflows

The water level in your pool will need topping up from time to time, particularly during a dry spell or if you are planning to have a moving water feature, as a certain amount of moisture is lost through evaporation. If the water level drops too much, fish and plants may suffer as well as the structure of the sides being damaged. You could plan for an automatic top-up system at construction stage. A chamber is fed by a mains water inlet and controlled by a ball valve like those found in toilet cisterns.

Should you expect the opposite problem – too much water, especially in winter – an overflow system would be sensible. This is particularly important with formal raised pools where any spillage would spoil paving and other features as well as damage the pond. You insert a pipe in the side at its lowest point and run it away at a gradient of no less than 1:80 into a drainage ditch. As a rough guide, a pool sized at around 215sq ft (20sq m) will need a pipe of 3in (7.5cm) diameter. A larger pool will require at least 4in (10cm) piping.

Pond Liners

Pre-Cast Fibreglass

Pre-cast pond moulds come in a wide range of shapes and sizes and a choice of colours. Some imitate complete features such as a waterfall, a watercourse or even a rocky pool. Properly installed and integrated, they are a simple and effective option for those

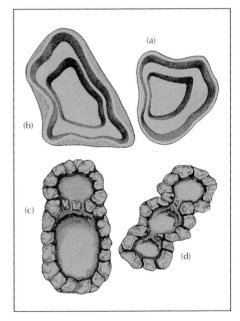

Selection of fibreglass moulds. (a) A small, simple mould with built-in shelf. (b) A larger informal pool with surrounding overlap, which is useful if you want to cover with soil. (c) Some moulds incorporate imitation rocks. (d) You can even buy a fibreglass mould that includes three levels and a watercourse.

Cool damp conditions are perfect for a collection of lush ferns which add a special highlight to any planting scheme with their feathery fronds. There are many different types, some of which can be planted in, or right at the edge of, the water, but most prefer a shady position. Ferns do not require much soil to root, but it should contain a high percentage of humus. Royal fern, *Omunda regalis*, is large and impressive, especially in autumn when the leaves change to a wonderful copper colour. Better suited to small pools are the fine arching fronds of the ostrich feather fern, *Matteuccia struthiopteris*, which is best planted in groups to show off the foliage and which prefers a rich soil in shade or semi-shade.

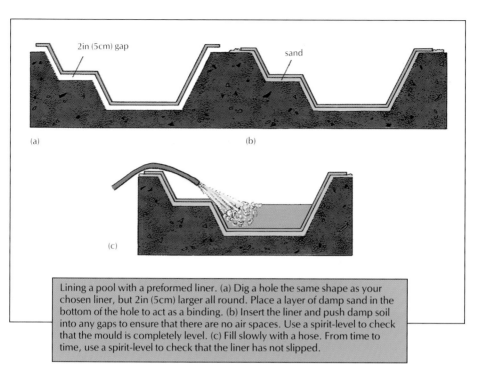

2in (5cm) gap

sand

(a)

(b)

(c)

Lining a pool with a preformed liner. (a) Dig a hole the same shape as your chosen liner, but 2in (5cm) larger all round. Place a layer of damp sand in the bottom of the hole to act as a binding. (b) Insert the liner and push damp soil into any gaps to ensure that there are no air spaces. Use a spirit-level to check that the mould is completely level. (c) Fill slowly with a hose. From time to time, use a spirit-level to check that the liner has not slipped.

who do not want the bother of a more adaptable liner and who can find exactly the size and shape they need. You simply excavate your hole to the shape of your mould, allowing 2in (5cm) extra on the depth and 4in (10cm) on the width and

You can buy a range of preformed pools at your local water garden centre, both formal and informal designs complete with marginal shelf.

length. Once you have checked for sharp stones, you need a base of 2in (5cm) of damp sand. The mould is eased gently down into position, taking care it does not get damaged, and any gaps are then packed with damp sand. Check that the top is absolutely level with a spirit-level. It is important to disguise the lipped top of the pool in some way and this is usually done using turves, stones or pavers.

Flexible Liners

A flexible liner is the most adaptable method of lining a pool and properly fitted is durable and attractive too. PVC (poly-vinyl chloride) is the least expensive and comes in varying grades which affects its longevity. Tougher, longer lasting and more expensive is rubber butyl.

Rubber pool liner partially fitted: the weight of the water will stretch it into place once the pool is filled from a slow hosepipe.

To estimate how much liner you need, calculate the length of your pool plus twice the maximum depth; the width will be the width plus twice the maximum depth. You do not need to allow for ledges and contours as the liner stretches to fit.

Leaving the liner in a warm room overnight helps it to be more flexible when you fit it. Remove the topsoil and turves from the immediate area around the pond to a depth of about 3in (7.5cm) to accommodate the overlap. The liner is then laid over the pool and weighted down with boulders, bricks or anything not likely to puncture the material. You then start to fill the pool using a hosepipe, allowing the water to trickle in slowly. As it fills, the weight of the water will stretch the liner into every contour, and you should help it by folding and tucking where necessary. When the pool is filled you can cut away any excess, leaving about 12in (30cm) to be concealed under your chosen edging material.

Concrete Lining

Concrete-lined pools are strong and watertight with the added advantage that you can stand in the bottom of them without fear of damage, which is useful for cleaning and maintenance work. Concrete also looks particularly good when used to construct

Section through a pond showing how the walls have slopes of at least 15 degrees to increase their strength. Special troughs have been built into the design to display marginal plants.

formal pools and watercourses. Until recently concrete was the only option, but it does need some skill – and hard work – to work with successfully, and with a pool the sides need to be at least 4in (10cm) thick to withstand the force of the water and possible freezing. Even with chemical additives concrete may well crack at extreme temperatures, although it is possible to repair it if you are able to drain the pool.

It is essential to measure all the ingredients accurately and to have had some experience of using concrete before. All but the smallest pools will require a concrete mixer, and you can measure the ingredients using a shovel or barrow. Large pools may require a delivery of ready mix, but do make sure you are ready for delivery as the mixture starts to set quickly. To calculate how much you will need, you add the surface area of the sides to that of the base and multiply by the thickness – 6in (15cm) is most usual.

Before concreting, the area must be covered with ¾in (19mm) chicken wire tied together with steel ties. The wire must be in good condition and not rusty. If you have sloped the sides, you will not need shuttering. Otherwise, hold this in place all round about 4in (10cm) from the sides and using 2 × 2in (5 × 5cm) stakes. The shuttering may be made from spare timber provided it is ½–1in (1–3cm) thick. Soaking in water or rubbing the shuttering with soap before adding the concrete helps it to be removed more easily later.

Concreting should never be carried out if the weather is very warm – it dries too quickly – or if it is frosty. Make up a strong concrete mix of one-part cement:three-parts sand:six-parts aggregate. Mix the dry ingredients well on a large plywood board then add enough water to create a stiff, porridge-like mix. Add any waterproofing, frostproofing and colouring chemicals as required. Apply the mixed concrete to the sides and base of the pool using a trowel

Shuttering for concrete-lined pools. Shuttering the sides in wood will help to keep the concrete in place until it has set. Position the shuttering around the sides of your excavation, allowing enough room for both the concrete and a layer of reinforcing chicken wire. Remove the wood when the concrete is dry.

and working it well into the chicken wire; provided the mix is stiff enough, it should not slump to the bottom. At the top, the concrete can be recessed into the bank with a 3in (7.5cm) notch. Any levelling pegs must be removed before the concrete is fully dry. Finally, smooth the surface to a fine finish using a float.

A tarpaulin or plastic sheet is useful to cover the cement and protect it should there be any risk of rain or frost – and also to protect it from strong sunlight, for the slower it dries the stronger it will be. You can fill the pond with water as soon as the initial hardening has taken place and it is dry to the touch. However, you cannot stock with plants or fish until the effects of the poisonous lime in the cement have been sluiced away by emptying and refilling the pool three or four times over several weeks. If you can, wait three months before stocking with fish and aquatic plants. You can buy a proprietary sealant to avoid waiting; it does wear off after a while, but the effects are minimal by then.

Clay Puddling

Where a pond or lake is too large for a liner or where you wish to create a totally authentic wildlife pool, the base and sides can be sealed with damp clay or chalk called clay puddling. Sometimes you may find suitable material occurring on site, but if not you can buy it in the form of a type of aluminium silicate more usually used to line reservoirs and canals – although it is quite expensive in large amounts. You can work small areas by hand using wooden boards or simply your hands and the soles of your boots, but with large ponds the digging machine is usually used to puddle the clay against the bottom and sides until a suitably waterproof bond is made. The idea is to build up thin layers of the puddled clay until a thickness of around 6in (15cm) is reached.

Raised Pools

Where you are planning a pool within an existing garden or paved patio, a raised pond may be a more practical option. It also looks good as part of a patio complex where it can be combined with raised beds, seating and other built-in features or used to create a change of level. If too dominant, it can be built in to a natural slope or an area of timber decking. Although expensive to build, it is perfect for disabled people who can observe fish and plants more easily.

A raised pool is usually circular or oval to withstand the pressure of water, although you do see interlocking squares and rectangles. Something strong is required to hold the pressure of water so concrete lining is preferred, although a fibreglass liner can be used provided there is a strong retaining wall. If you have any doubts, seek professional help. A raised pool is usually faced in brick or stone to match other features in the vicinity.

Raised pools are less likely than other water features to be affected by any local

A raised pool often fits very well within a formal patio design. Materials for the pool surround can be chosen to match or co-ordinate with those of the paved area, as well as other features that are part of the water garden complex.

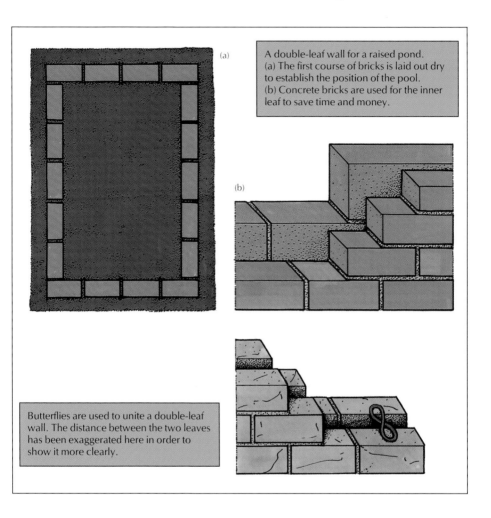

(a)

A double-leaf wall for a raised pond.
(a) The first course of bricks is laid out dry to establish the position of the pool.
(b) Concrete bricks are used for the inner leaf to save time and money.

(b)

Butterflies are used to unite a double-leaf wall. The distance between the two leaves has been exaggerated here in order to show it more clearly.

planning rules or restrictions, but it is best to check before you start building.

Sink and Tub Pools

Provided it is waterproof, any attractive container such as an old sink, stone trough, wooden barrel or even a large terracotta pot could be used to create a small self-contained water feature as an additional focal-point in the garden or on the patio. The only drawback is that because of its size and exposed nature, the water is likely to freeze solid in winter. The best solution to this problem is to overwinter plants and fish in an aquarium.

Your container should be at least 9in (22.5cm) deep with any drainage holes well sealed. Glazed objects such as sinks can be given a more natural appearance by priming with glue then adding a mixture of

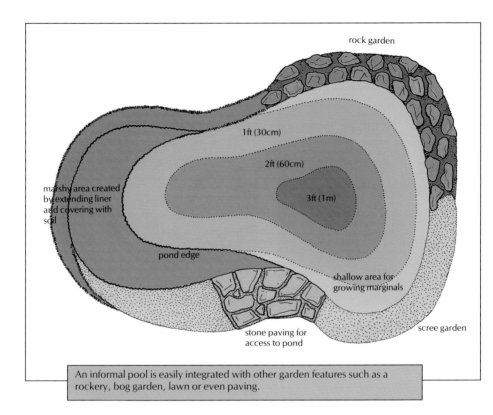

rock garden

1ft (30cm)

2ft (60cm)

3ft (1m)

marshy area created by extending liner and covering with soil

pond edge

shallow area for growing marginals

stone paving for access to pond

scree garden

An informal pool is easily integrated with other garden features such as a rockery, bog garden, lawn or even paving.

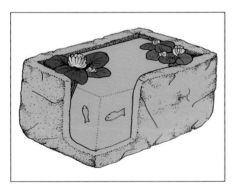

An old stone sink or wooden tub makes a super miniature pool to support dwarf water-lilies and a few fish. The pool might be free standing on the patio or in the garden, or it may be sunk into the ground.

two-parts cement:one-part peat:four-parts sand. Such a small container may be limited in scope, but you can still enjoy one of the miniature water-lilies and a few fish. A selection of interesting pool-side plants may be arranged nearby in similar containers. Some patio containers are suitable for adapting to a moving water feature: you can buy terracotta urns with small fountains already fitted which make a most attractive feature either indoors or out.

3 • POOL EDGES AND PLANTS

You could easily ruin a perfectly good pool simply by not bothering to finish it off properly. It is important that you plan the immediate pond surroundings as carefully as every other aspect of the feature since your chosen finish will not only hide the liner, but also highlight or soften the outline of the pool, depending on which treatment you choose, and help it to sit well in its surroundings. An edging could be formal or informal, or a mixture of the two if you prefer it and are confident the combination could work with your pond. Informal might mean simply that you re-lay the turves over your chosen lining material where it overlaps the bank. Of course, the most natural effect would combine suitable water-loving plants with the grass and this is a popular choice for an informally-shaped pool.

You should aim at a range of different types of plant from the aquatics in the water to the dramatic marginals on their shelf and moisture-preferring bog plants close to the pool (see Plants page 28). You will want to leave part of the area free of plants so that you can actually get to the pool and observe

The liner must be concealed behind some kind of edging material. Here random stone can be arranged to overhang the pool edge as well as keep the gravel path contained.

Smooth round pebbles suitable for pool edgings and oriental designs are available from good garden and water garden centres.

it at closer quarters, and turf is perfect here – or perhaps you might consider a shingle beach sloping down into the water (this is a decision you should make before the pool is constructed). In some locations, a carefully positioned collection of rocks or boulders is most in keeping with the rest of the garden. If you are using plants to surround your pool, do make sure they are positioned appropriately according to their height and spread: tall stately subjects like reeds and iris at the back, large-leaved marginals giving weight to the side, and towards you as you view the pool the shorter often ground-hugging species like water forget-me-nots and *Geums*.

Bog Gardens

A bog garden is the most natural extension from your pool; it makes a good overflow facility and is perfect for integrating the

A mature but well-maintained informal pool, with a pebble beach and a fine stand of yellow flag iris.

One of the pleasures of owning a pool or pond is the chance to grow some interesting reeds and rushes which come in a wide variety of colours and patterns. One of the most striking is the zebra rush, sometimes called the porcupine quill rush, *Scirpus tabernaemontani zebrinus*, which produces unusual cream and white horizontally striped markings up the stem. This hardy plant will grow well in shallow water, provided it receives plenty of sunshine. Any plain green stems which develop should be cut out to prevent the plant reverting.

feature with the rest of the garden. Again, this is best installed at the same time as the pool, simply extending the liner over the desired area at a depth of around 14in (35cm). The bog garden should not extend to more than 10 to 15 per cent of the total surface area of the pool. The bottom of the liner should be punctured with small drainage holes – about one hole per 3sq ft (1sq m) – to produce the desired effect of waterlogged soil; that is, with around 2–3in (7.5cm) of water standing on top of the soil. A few holes ½in (13mm) in diameter in the dividing wall between pond and bog should cope with top-up and drainage requirements during any fluctuation in the weather in winter.

Where a bog garden is independent of a pool, you will have to provide separate overflow facilities to a nearby ditch and top it up with a hose as necessary. To make this job more efficient, it helps to lay a section of plastic pipe on top of the lining material in the bottom of the feature. You should punch holes in the pipe at about 24in (60cm) intervals then attach the other end to a hosepipe when required. The other end of the pipe is easily hidden when the bog garden is planted.

Formal Edgings

A formal edging is an obvious choice for a formal pool, whether raised or sunken, on a patio or part of the garden scheme. Yet slabs, brick and stone can look very

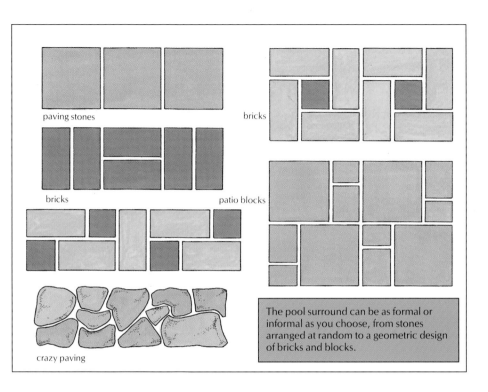

paving stones

bricks

bricks

patio blocks

crazy paving

The pool surround can be as formal or informal as you choose, from stones arranged at random to a geometric design of bricks and blocks.

effective surrounding an informal shape too; sometimes the paving units are embedded in grass to soften the effect slightly. Deciding which type to have can be difficult as there are so many shapes, colours and sizes, but obviously it will have to be something that matches, or at least co-ordinates with, other hard landscaping features nearby such as a wall, patio, raised beds or built-in seating area. Whatever you choose, you must check that the bricks, tiles or paving are specifically produced for outdoor use and will be able to withstand hard frost and rain. You may wish to build up the area slightly and use coping stones on top to create a wider, level place to sit and observe the plants and wildlife. Within a patio complex, the pool may be integrated with planting areas, seating and other features anyway. Other, less frequently-used

paving materials that could be used around a pond area include old railway sleepers, well-preserved log slices set in turf for a setting with a woodland atmosphere, and stone or granite kerbstones, the kind more often used in road construction.

Timber Decking

A popular and immensely practical design feature that is being used increasingly to surround pools is timber decking. It can be laid in formal designs and extended to include all kinds of ancillary features, yet always retains a soft, very natural feel about it. Allow the pool to disappear beneath a timber decked patio area and it will seem much larger than it really is. The deck could be extended to build seating, paths, even an overhead pergola. A low-level deck no more than 3ft 3in (1m) off the ground is simple to erect provided the ground is firm and level. A higher-level deck and anything constructed on boggy or unstable ground should only be erected after seeking professional advice.

The deck is supported on 4 × 4in (10 × 10cm) or 6 × 6in (15 × 15cm) wooden posts, depending on the distance to be spanned by the bearer timbers which will be 3 × 4in (7.5 × 10cm) to 4 × 6in (10 × 15cm). The support posts must not be built more than 6ft (1.8m) apart and the horizontal joists 3–4ft (1–1.2m) apart.

Timbers used in the deck construction must be hardwoods given at least two coats of preservative and an annual top-up. The wood for the walking surface is usually 1 × 2in (2.5 × 5cm), 1 × 3in (2.5 × 7.5cm) or even 1 × 4in (2.5 × 10cm) with slightly bevelled edges for a smart finish. Softwoods can be used here but they are prone to splintering and require regular maintenance.

You can lay the decking planks in a variety of interesting patterns and designs, such as weaves and zig-zags. Patterns are more time-consuming to erect than straight, parallel courses as every time the wood changes direction it must be nailed down and this means providing supporting timber at these points. Galvanized nails and screws are best for all fixings and the screw heads should be countersunk.

A safety rail is a good idea where a deck overhangs a pool and this is easily made by extending the support posts and fixing bamboo poles, thick ship's rope or rounded timber at least 3in (7.5cm) in diameter.

You can leave planting spaces for the kind of plants you would normally find close to a pool – contained, they will be easier to control and maintain; or grow them in tubs, pots and boxes strategically positioned on the decking surface.

The flowering rush, *Butomus umbellatus*, is a native of Europe and Asia and thrives in water up to 4in (10cm) deep. It enjoys an open sunny position and produces attractive sword-shaped leaves which can be any colour from purple to green. Pale to reddish pink flower heads like upside-down umbrellas appear in midsummer with as many as 30 flowers on a single stalk, and it is for this display that the plant is mainly grown in garden pools. You can propagate this deciduous plant by seed in spring or late summer, or by division in spring.

Plants for the Water Garden

Lush, large-leaved species, tall spiky plants and, of course, the lovely water-lily epitomize some of the delights of owning a pond or indeed any water feature. Even if you only have room for one or two, or they have to be grown in containers to be positioned near to rather than in the pool, they offer an

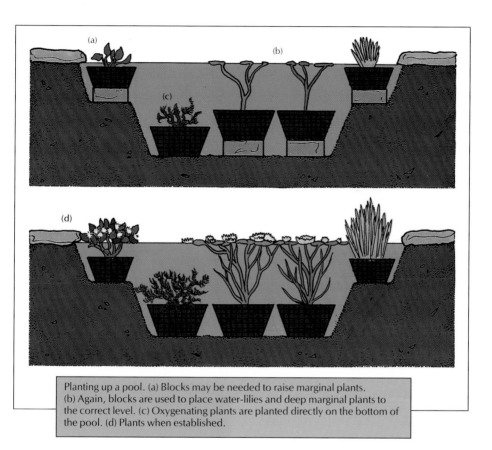

Planting up a pool. (a) Blocks may be needed to raise marginal plants.
(b) Again, blocks are used to place water-lilies and deep marginal plants to
the correct level. (c) Oxygenating plants are planted directly on the bottom of
the pool. (d) Plants when established.

exciting, almost exotic addition to the garden or patio.

Generally speaking, water plants are easy to look after; they are not particularly fussy about soil and situation provided the conditions are moist and not in complete shade. Most tend to be rather rampant growers and will need plenty of compost during the growing season and a good cut-back or prune before they die back for the winter.

There is a wonderful variety of plants to choose from and it is tempting to buy too many and end up with an overcrowded display – all those prolific growers jostling for space. It is preferable to have a smaller

This tiny pool has certainly maximized its potential with a wonderful variety of poolside shapes and colours; within the pool itself are darting fish and spiky water soldier (Stratiotes aloides).

An attractively planted informal pond which is well controlled despite its very natural appearance, with an easy–to–maintain stone and turf surround and marginal plants in a striking blend of golds and greens.

but carefully chosen selection that provides a good contrast of sizes and leaf shapes. Start by choosing a few of those plants that earn their keep – the pond oxygenators. These grow on the water's surface and should never be allowed to cover more than a third of the pool's volume. They grow fast and furious but most are highly attractive too – simply weight the stems and drop to the bottom of the pool. Water violet (*Hottonia palustris*) has pretty green fern-like leaves and pale mauve flowers; water starwort (*Callitriche palustris*) as its name suggests is an attractive star shape; milfoil (*Myriophyllum spicatum*) is a fine purifier and an attractive sight too – reddish stems, whorls of olive green leaves and, in summer, tiny red and yellow flowers.

Some aquatic plants simply float on the surface so are just popped into the water. They need a water depth of between 12-36in (30-90cm). This group includes frogbit

A plant which produces a long and continuous display of flowers is always welcome. *Sisynchium brachypus*, also known as dwarf golden-eyed grass, sprinkles its grass-like tufty clumps with bright yellow flowers through spring and summer. Semi-evergreen, this is a plant that prefers sun although it will tolerate partial shade and enjoys the moist soil close to a pond or pool. It can be propagated by division in early spring or by seed in spring or autumn.

(*Hydrocharis morsus-ranae*), a hardy perennial with distinctive kidney-shaped leaves and tiny white flowers like a miniature water lily, and the very different spiky water soldier (*Stratiotes aloides*) which looks rather like the top of a pineapple floating on the water.

You will want at least one water-lily, of course. There are, however, dwarf varieties if you are short of space. All are beautiful, the classic blooms opening out above those strange disc-like leaves. They require plenty of rich compost, which is usually packed into a special container or old milk crate and lowered to the bottom of the pool. The leaves should rise and just rest on the surface of the water; if the stem is not long enough, you may have to stand the

This semi-formal pool with its wonderful display of water-lilies uses a good variety of foliage and flowers in planting spaces close to the water's edge and in pots to soften an old stone edging.

Water-lilies prefer still water where they can create a thick carpet of disc-like leaves and breathtakingly beautiful blooms. For easier maintenance they are best planted in wire baskets which are positioned at the bottom of the pool. Most pond or pool owners yearn after at least one or two water-lilies, but they are invasive so your choice will be restricted. There is no limit to the scope and variety of the flowers which might be any colour from pink and red to yellow and white in a variety of petalled forms; leaves might be red tinted, finely marked or mottled. For small pools, there is a dwarf variety *Nymphaea pygmaea alba* which needs only enough water to cover the crown and produces white flowers 1½in (3.5cm) across.

container on bricks or a similar support; but do make sure it is something that cannot damage the pond liner.

The blooms can vary quite considerably not just in colour but in shape too. There are star-shaped varieties, open types, globes and some with petals like a dahlia. Most take the family name *Nymphaea* and can be either tender or hardy. Most open when the sun is out and some are even scented: *Nymphaea odorata*, for example. The variety 'Helvola' is supposedly the smallest of all the water lilies and needs a depth of only 9–12in (20-30cm). Water-lilies and other base-rooted, floating aquatics are usually planted in wire or plastic mesh baskets, which enable the plant to be removed more easily for maintenance. Plants can be arranged in groups in larger containers or an old milk crate. The container should be lined first with turf to help prevent the compost washing away; this should be rich and heavy like silt. Stones or pebbles on top of the soil prevent fish disturbing it. Take care how you lower containers into the pool as they will be heavy and could do a lot of damage if you let one slip. It is important that the containers are positioned so that the leaves just float on the surface of the water, so they may have to be propped up on weighted blocks, taking care not to damage the lining material and ensuring that they are stable.

Moving further towards the edge of the pond are the marvellous marginals – those dramatic species you can plant around your marginal shelf. Many have large or boldly-shaped foliage; a small pool or stream will only have room for a few, so make sure you choose a good balance of shapes – something tall and spiky like a reed or rush; something with outsize leaves: perhaps a *Petasites japonica*; and other contrasting shapes such as thick fleshy hostas, the marsh marigold's mass of golden blooms, or the arrow-shaped leaves of a *Sagittaria*.

Marginal plants can be planted directly on the pond shelf by backfilling with soil and fronting with large rocks or stones to prevent them slipping into the water. They must be planted at the same level as they were in the pot or nursery bed. Alternatively, marginals can be planted in the same kind of open mesh container as aquatic plants and these propped up on the shelf with a boulder or two to prevent them slipping off.

Out of the water but still preferring moist conditions are the kind of plants you find in boggy areas beside a pool or stream. Hardy *Astilbes* are useful for their mass of colourful plume-like flowers; you can grow frondy ferns, exotic-looking grasses and bamboos, glamorous iris, ground-hugging creeping jenny with its carpet of star-shaped flowers or, for spring, a display of wonderful primula.

To plant out, you should first remove the specimen from its hessian wrapping, pot or container and measure its root size. Dig a hole about four times this size, keeping the topsoil to use again. Water the plant well

For a really exotic touch in or around a pond or pool, the wild South African lily, *Zantedeschia aethiopica*, produces spectacular waxy white blooms against arrow shaped, deep green leaves. Also called the Arum lily, the flowers appear in summer and the plant requires full sun and a well-drained soil, although it will tolerate partial shade. It is ideal for town gardens which tend to be warmer and more sheltered, as it is only frost hardy to 50°F (10°C). You can lift the plants to be overwintered in a frost-free greenhouse. Arum lily can be propagated from offsets taken in winter.

and spread the roots out a little before lowering carefully into the planting hole. Make sure the plant is planted at the same level as it was before. Fill in the hole with compost or your reserved topsoil mixed with organic matter, firm gently and water in.

4 • MOVING WATER FEATURES

For a small investment, an electric pump will add a new dimension to your water garden plans or indeed to your whole garden scheme. The movement, light and soothing sounds supplied by a fountain, cascade, waterfall or water spout, can enhance your garden or patio as well as providing hours of pleasure. Water is less likely to freeze solid if the pump is kept running, and the splashing water produces oxygen which is good for wildlife. Bear in mind, however, that while fish will be attracted by the extra oxygen, they prefer to live in still waters and that plants too prefer an unruffled pool. This is particularly true of water lilies which will not thrive near a fountain or falls.

Whether you choose a simple feature or

A simple plume fountain adds sparkle and life to the smallest pool.

Lead flashing and a tile are used to create a curtain-effect cascade between formal brick pools.

an elaborate one, there are other practical points to be considered first. If the water flows too fast, or too slow, the feature will not operate properly. The larger the feature, the greater the volume of water to circulate so the right size pump must be purchased, especially if you are using one pump to run a couple of features such as a waterfall and a fountain by fixing a T-piece to the outlet pipe. A stream that is too wide will flow too fast and spill over the sides, whereas a too-tall waterfall may not be able to recycle the

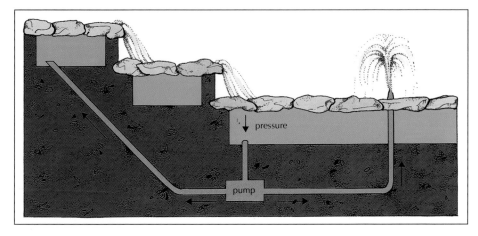

Provided it has sufficient power, a surface pump can be used to run a selection of moving water features simultaneously. Here, a fountain and watercourse are powered by one pump.

water fast enough. Fountains must be the right size for their pools or too much water may splash over the sides or be blown by the wind and need replacing too frequently.

There are basically two types of pumps. Surface pumps are positioned outside the pool but near to it and need some kind of housing to protect them from the weather. This has to be concealed somehow behind plants or boulders yet still remain accessible for maintenance. Underwater or submersible pumps are positioned on a permanent level surface in the pool itself where there is no risk of the inlet becoming exposed which could create an airlock in the system. The pump should not be placed too deep; the largest amount of lift is best arranged above water level. Submersible pumps are to be preferred – not simply because they are easier to maintain and to conceal, but they are also more economical to run and can produce an output of up to 1,000 gallons (4,500 litres) per hour with a head of water (that is, the height of the cascade above the water level of the pool) of approximately 3ft (1m).

Installing the pump should present no problems: once the pump has been positioned, the outlet pipe is connected to the

Naturally found in damp meadows, the globeflower, *Trollius europaeus* is easily recognized by its clumps of bright yellow, globe-shaped blooms from early to late summer. The fresh green leaves are equally appealing, being palmate and deeply cut. It will do well in the moist soil beside pools and streams provided it is well drained, and it will tolerate sun or shade. The plant is best propagated by division in early autumn or by seed in summer or autumn.

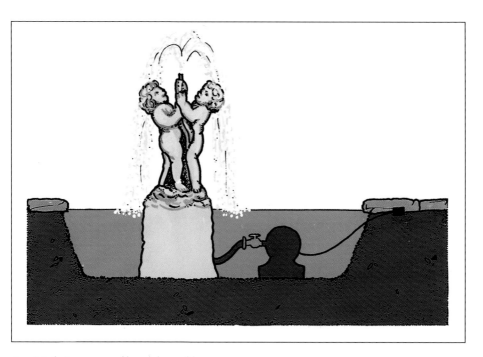

Fountain feature powered by a submersible pump.

Waterfall and fountain powered by an above-ground pump.

Formal garden pools on different levels might be linked by a simple outlet pipe. A small electric pump circulates water back to the top pool. These interlocking geometric designs have been built in brick and lined with a paint-on pond sealant.

top of the waterfall or base of the fountain fitting and the armoured cable run to the nearest electrical point. This is best buried underground inside a plastic conduit where it is less likely to be encountered by an unwary spade. All plugs and fittings ought to be waterproof and recommended for outside use. If you are in any doubt, consult a qualified electrician.

Fountains

Fountains have the potential to be one of the most elaborate water features and certainly the most exciting, with the option of abstract and figurative ornaments incorporated in the display, and changing lights, even music orchestrated into a changing sequence of different fountain effects. Some are more tasteful than others and it is up to you to decide what will suit you and your garden best. They are certainly useful for adding height to a scheme and for creating an eye-catching focal-point.

In many ways, the simple plumes of water are more stunning as there is nothing to distract the eye from the water, but various effects are possible including a circular curtain of spray; a foaming jet which produces a large foaming column of white water rather than individual jet sprays; the volcano types where the water appears in several tiered layers of individual sprays; adjustable calyx forms; plus domes and 'bells' of water which produce the appearance of a three-dimensional solid shape. Many of these effects are adjustable or several fountain types can be linked in sequence to produce a changing display. Classical yet still simple enough to suit most schemes is the familiar three-tier bowl effect constructed from ceramic or concrete where the water cascades freely from one bowl to another.

For a wholly original look, you might consider a water sculpture, bearing in mind that you will be purchasing a piece of art and this will be reflected in the price. It may

This very formal pool relies on a pair of fountain figures and a limited selection of plants for interest. Too many rampant pool-edge plants would have ruined the important shape and relevance of the pool in this instance.

An ornate free-standing fountain makes an eye-catching feature for garden or patio and could not be simpler to install.

be an abstract piece such as a tubular pyramid of shiny silver metal, punctured at intervals to produce a fine criss-cross spray; or a young girl in bronze just dipping her toe in the water. You must be careful how you position such a piece; most look best with a backdrop of plants or unobtrusive trellis or screening to focus attention on the sculpture. Sometimes interesting foliage plants can be used close by for their softening effect and to provide bold contrasts.

For smaller gardens and patios, fountains can still be creative in the shape of simple water spouts pouring from decorative wall heads, an old tap or pump handle, or from bubble fountains where the water spills over an orb, an old millstone or similar object into a hidden reservoir below. The beauty of all these features is not just that they take up very little room, but that they are safer for young children too. Basic display fountains simply connect the pump to the fountain nozzle or jet via a length of plastic tubing of the correct diameter and jubilee clips. The nozzle or jet should be supported just clear of the water's surface. With ornamental and sculpture fountain features, the tubing connects to an integral pipe. For a bubble fountain, you need to sink the reservoir concealing the pump below ground and position the water spout at ground level at the centre of your chosen feature. As with pools, the reservoir should not be less than twice the height of the proposed fountain jet. It is also important to make sure the water does not splash over the sides beyond the reservoir, resulting in damage to the surrounding area and inconvenient water loss.

A bubble fountain can foam over an attractive arrangement of pebbles, an old millstone or iron ball with no risk to young children as the reservoir is completely concealed underground.

Rushes, reeds and sedges are traditional pond-edge plants and they can offer an exciting variety of foliage shapes: not just spikes and pokers but also glossy green spiders like evergreen sedge, *Cyperus*. Commonly called umbrella grass on account of the distinctive shape of its leaves, this popular marginal plant produces graceful stems of bright green 'umbrellas' decorated with brown umbrels in summer. There are various varieties, including a white-striped variegated type, all of which are frost tender.

Waterfalls and Cascades

A large waterfall would not be practical — nor look very natural — in the majority of gardens; it would be extremely difficult and costly to construct, and the volume of water to be circulated would not be feasible. However, a more modest natural falls as part of a rockery feature or a formal cascade incorporated into a formal pool complex is extremely successful and relatively easy to build. You may have a hilly area or change of level within your garden that suggests such a feature and this will help it look more at home in its surroundings. An informal waterfall cascading over rocks and boulders is often planned in conjunction with a pool and the mound partly constructed using the waste from the pool excavation. Getting the boulders to look

Studying the different types of waterfall in the wild will help you to achieve an authentic effect when building your own in the garden.

A prefabricated cascade can be used to create an informal look.

just right is tricky, so be prepared for considerable trial and error until you are happy that it looks natural. Certainly do not mortar any rocks into position until you are absolutely sure it is right. It helps to choose large rocks rather than small ones, to tilt them slightly backwards when they are bedded in and to take note of the natural strata of the stone. They can look good as part of a rockery, but you should line the back of the falls with butyl so that water is not lost down the back. Even so, larger waterfalls will need a top-up tank to replace water lost from splashing and evaporation. You can buy fibreglass preformed waterfalls or cascades to be concealed between the boulders, but the rocks should still be lined. Moisture-loving plants with bold foliage like bamboo and *Fatsia japonica* are useful for disguising and softening the edges of the waterfall and for providing extra height at the top.

For the patio or formal garden, a cascade is more in keeping. A series of steps or weirs

Gold or yellow plants or those with golden markings are useful for adding variety and interest to a planting scheme, or for making a splash of brightness among all those lush green shapes. Few plants do this as efficiently as *Carex stricta* 'Bowles Golden', a really eye-catching sedge, perfect as the focal-point along the edge of a lake or stream. Growing to a height of around 12in (30cm), it produces a shaggy clump of bright yellow foliage making an excellent backdrop for fleshier green plants, or as a foreground feature against a green backdrop of trees or shrubs.

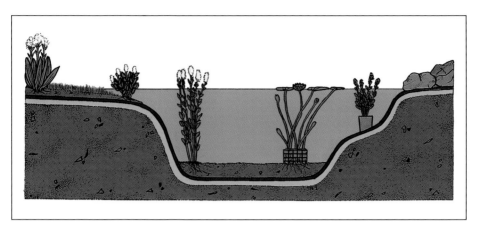

Ideally, an informal pond should incorporate a range of depths: a deep area to prevent the water from freezing in winter and shallows to attract wildlife and grow a variety of marginal plants.

is a popular feature and can be constructed from any waterproof paving material such as stone, slabs or bricks to co-ordinate with their surroundings. Often a cascade is a useful device to link two or more formal pools on different levels. Another idea is to have the water flowing down the face of a brick or perspex wall, with fins or protruding bricks adding variety and interest.

With both waterfalls and cascades, you may experience a problem with water seeping down the back of the overhang and trickling along the vertical face instead of making a curtain effect. This can be resolved by providing a lip or ledge at the top, which can be a concrete slab, timber or invisible perspex depending on the style of the feature. If you have problems at the top with water trickling down the side of the outlet pipe, this is usually because the pipe has been positioned to the side; moving it to the top of the feature should resolve this.

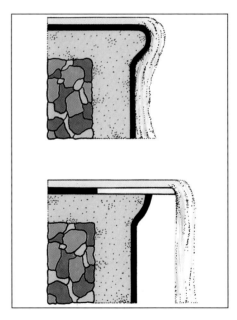

Improving a waterfall or cascade. Water tends to flow down the back of the overhang. This can be remedied by inserting a small perspex lip, tile or slab to project the curtain of water away from the back wall.

Streams and Watercourses

The snaking qualities of a stream or slender

This natural stream edge features carefully arranged natural rocks and waterside plants such as the striking skunk cabbage Lysichitum americanum *whose large green leaves and bright yellow arum-like flowers materialize out of the mud in spring.*

profile of a watercourse are excellent for using your water feature to reshape (visually at least) your garden plot or to divide it into new areas. Alternatively use one to link two ponds or a formal and informal water feature. It need not be wide, nor very deep – 1½in (4cm) is fine, just enough to bubble merrily over a bed of pebbles. A natural-style stream with banks all moss and boulders is, like the waterfall, a matter of observing nature and a lot of trial and error. Water always takes the line of least resistance, flowing round solid obstacles, so use large boulders to indicate a change of course. Rocks, pools and weirs can all be used to add interest and change the pace of the water. Soften the edges with a selection of marginal plants and, if the stream is big enough, incorporate bridges or stepping-

A stream effect has been used to divide one area of the garden from another, with access via a sturdy but attractive wickerwork bridge adding an air of secrecy and expectation to the garden area beyond.

A novel idea for a water feature: a narrow stone-edged stream partially encloses an island bed of bright annuals.

stones at logical crossing points. A man-made stream does not slope but uses a pump to move the water, otherwise it would all run to the bottom in one rush and have to wait to be pumped up again. If the site is naturally sloping, you will have to allow for this by terracing and building in a series of weirs. As it is, you will have to select a pump powerful enough to take the volume of water up to the top again.

A stream or watercourse is constructed more or less the same way as you would a pool (*see* page 15) and the banks kept strictly level. If the stream is a rather winding one, you will have to hire a special instrument called an optical level. Straight streams and watercourses can be levelled by setting up a levelling post measuring 4ft (1.2m) at the start of your mapped-out shape. Place a second post 10ft (3m) away in line with the direction of the stream, making sure it is level with the first by checking with your straight-edge and spirit-level. A third post should be positioned at the far end of the stream and a length of fishing-line stretched between all three to check that they are in a straight line. Do not allow the line to actually touch the middle post or it will deflect it slightly and spoil your calculations. Make yourself a

The distinctive arrow-shaped leaves of hardy *Sagittaria sagittifolia* make a handsome contrast to the spikes and fronds of many other marginal plants. You will often see it in the wild alongside rivers and in pond shallows, displaying large white flowers with black centres. There is a cultivar *S. s* 'Flore Pleno' whose flowers are particularly lovely and which blooms all summer. Equally hardy is the larger leaved and even more dramatic *S. japonica* whose beautiful white flowers can be up to 2in (5cm) across.

The false bulrush, *Typha latifolia*, is a classic for ponds and lakes with its grey-green spiky leaves and tall brown pokers. The pokers appear in autumn following the spikes of beige flowers. Like many marginals, this deciduous perennial plant is invasive and needs careful control if it is not to take over other species. Its large clumps and vigorous habit makes it really only suitable for larger ponds and lakes, but there is a smaller version *T. minima* which only grows to 30in (75cm) in height and is perfect for smaller gardens.

T-shaped rod, its height calculated as that from the ground to the top of the post plus the depth of the proposed stream excavation – usually 24in (60cm). Use this as a guide to excavation, making sure that as you dig down it remains level with the line at the top.

A watercourse is far more formal and might take the form of a moat, designed to make an island of a seating area or flower beds within the garden, or of miniature canals breaking up the garden into more interesting shapes. A watercourse can be lined in compressed clay, concrete or flexible liner and the sides constructed from concrete, brick, turf or timber.

5 • ADDITIONAL FEATURES AND WILDLIFE

As well as the pond, pool or water feature itself and the wonderful range of plants you will be able to grow in and around it, there are a great many ornaments and other related features to choose from. Even within a large water garden two or three is more than ample; any more and it begins to look like a fairy grotto. The style of your feature will determine to a large extent what you choose. For the oriental garden there are fake stone pagodas, *ishi doro* lanterns, lion dogs and Buddhas. A classical Greek goddess may be more your style, or a smaller ornament such as a stone or terracotta tortoise, frog or otter. Decorative urns come in all shapes and sizes from stone and terracotta to timber and fibreglass. These might be plain or ornately decorated with figures, fruit and flowers and are perfect for lush, moisture-loving plants, bamboos or a bright display of seasonal plants contained and easy to manage, yet close to the water. It is a good idea to have somewhere to sit close to your water feature so that you can observe plants and wildlife at your leisure. If you have not planned any built-in seating,

The tiniest formal round pool has been transformed into a witty joke with this Excalibur sculpture.

a simple timber bench or stone seat should transform even a small pool into a contemplative area.

Crossing the Water

A large pool or stream, or perhaps just a strategically placed stretch of water, offers the chance to incorporate a bridge or stepping stones into your overall water garden scheme. They need not be crossing deep water – a couple of inches is sufficient – but they will still give you a sense of moving into another part of the garden which adds an air of excitement and possibly mystery to even the smallest plot. Simple or ornate, the important thing is that they are functional, not simply decorative; nothing looks worse than an elaborate bridge which does not lead anywhere.

Stepping-stones should be put in position before the water is added. They can be made of any kind of paving material from slabs and log slices to sections of timber decking and random stones. They should be spaced so that even those with shorter legs can cross comfortably and safely and

An ornamental iron grille erected over a pool creates both an interesting feature and a safety device to prevent children and pets from falling into the water.

Even the smallest garden can feature a handsome bridge if the pool is carefully designed to suit its location. Most importantly, the bridge should go somewhere even if it is simply an island or small secluded area of your garden.

be positioned in such a way that they meander across, rather than going direct. You may prefer to sketch out their progress first on paper. Stones and concrete slabs could be fixed in concrete if preferred and all stepping-stones should be kept free from moss and algae growth to prevent them becoming slippery and dangerous.

Bridges are more complicated and expensive to construct, especially if you want an arched style – which is only really necessary if you need something high enough for boats to go under. They need to be level, non-slippery and at least wide enough to cross comfortably, that is a minimum of 24in (60cm). Bear in mind that it may have to be wide enough to take your mower or wheelbarrow too. Often simply using a long stone slab, a section of tree trunk or a plank placed casually across a narrow stream will suffice. Unless the area to be crossed is large, simply designed

bridges do look best and up to 8ft (2.4m) can be spanned before additional support is required. This usually takes the form of piers driven into the bed of the stream or watercourse using a special pile-driving machine. The piers must be at least 4 × 4in (10 × 10cm). The bridge itself might be a series of staggered planks or planked platforms, just skimming the water's surface and perfect for observing fish and plants.

Timber can be adapted to look both rustic and formal. Stain the wood soft shades of green, blue or grey for something a little more unusual; or a bright Chinese red if it makes a good focal-point within an oriental garden. All timber must be treated with preservative annually and only hardwoods used where it might be in direct contact with the water.

You can construct a single span bridge quite simply by driving in joist-supporting posts on both banks; a line stretched between the two and checked with a spirit-level will ensure they are level. To these are joined 4 × 4in (10 × 10cm) timber joists with 2 × 4in (5 × 10cm) or 2 × 6in (5 × 15cm) timber planking fastened at right angles with 3½in (9cm) screws or 4 × 6in (10 × 15cm) nails to create a level surface.

A handrail is a good idea for safety, especially if the bridge will be used by children or the elderly. It can be made from 2 × 2in (5 × 5cm) timber or 3in (7.5cm) diameter poles, regularly treated with a non-toxic preservative. If you like, you could fill in the spaces between the supporting timbers with a pattern of matching poles, decorative trellis or chicken wire for extra safety.

Ideally a bridge should match other hard landscaping features around the garden; but if a stone bridge – usually incorporating a central pier or keystone – is beyond your talents and your purse, consider a brick structure. Usually the bridge will be one or two shallow arches supported on concrete piers, with water plants grown to disguise the concrete footings. A concrete bridge is an expensive specialist job, but you can make your own by using a culvert or large concrete pipe as an instant support. It must be large enough to handle the volume of water or in peak periods this might wash the bridge away, or at best, erode it. You will have to divert or dam the stream while it is being installed. First, a concrete block is built on the stream bed, then the culvert (which may have been made to order) is lowered on to it. You can backfill the sides with hardcore or shutter them and fill with concrete. The whole structure can then be faced with brick or stone to make it look more attractive.

Lighting

Any kind of water feature benefits from being lit at night and as part of a

A simple timber bridge with handrail for safety crosses quite a wide stretch of water to lead from the garden to open countryside beyond. Raising the bridge using steps avoids having to build a far more complicated and expensive arched style of bridge.

comprehensive garden lighting scheme must surely create one of its most important focal-points after dark. It means you can enjoy your garden longer, indeed for most of the year since you will be able not only to sit out and enjoy parties and barbecues in summer but also appreciate the garden from

A large flat stone cemented to pillars (made of stone fragments) makes a simple but attractive bridge over a narrow stretch of water.

A small ornamental pool is only one of a series of formal garden features incorporated in this sophisticated lighting plan.

the comfort of your own armchair through patio windows in the colder months. Care needs to be taken when highlighting water as glare can be a problem; but there is usually plenty of opportunity to spotlight surrounding features such as dramatic marginal plants like *Gunnera*, or bridges, fountains and statuary. A mixture of lighting effects works best, especially if you can operate them independently so that you have a choice of effects. Beware of using too many garish coloured lights, often supplied in kits specially recommended for water gardens, as they can create too unsubtle an effect. Most importantly, the installation must be safe, so do get the advice of a qualified electrician unless you are absolutely sure of what you are doing.

The power supply to your lights can be combined with the services supplying other electrical features such as pumps and filters, but you will have to assess the power load per cable as there is a limit to how much you can load on to it. The larger spotlights are between 150W and 300W and the number your cable can hold is controlled by the power requirement of the lights and the distance the cable has to run. Several cables may be necessary or a thicker main cable. All cable for exterior use should be protected by a plastic conduit and buried at least 18in (46cm) in the ground so that it is not chanced upon by an unlucky spade or fork. If this is not possible, the cable might be run along a garden wall where it can be clipped out of reach within the mortar pointing using special fixing clips. All exterior wiring should be fitted with a residual current-operated circuit breaker (RCCB) which cuts out at the slightest deviation in the current reaching the earth.

To get some idea of the kind of effects you might achieve, it is worth taking a spotlight out on an exterior extension cable and shining it in different positions. You will find that bold planting looks best lit from

A selection of outdoor lamps and spotlights can be used to highlight the poolside.

Perennial purple loosestrife, *Lythrum salicaria*, grows quickly beside ponds and streams or in bog gardens, producing a clump of bright red/purple flower spikes around 4–5ft (1.2–1.5m) high. The leaves, carried on the flower stems, are small and lance-shaped. Fully hardy, it will tolerate full sun or semi-shade and prefers a moist, even wet, soil. It spreads quickly and is an excellent, easy-to-grow subject for bog gardens. Cultivars can be propagated by division in spring; species by seed or division in spring or autumn.

below and its lit reflection can be caught in the water's surface of a pond as an alternative to using underwater lights. Special features also look good picked out with a ground-spiked uplighter or a soft downlighter fastened to a wall or tree: sculptures or statues make an excellent focal-point, as does the 'white water' in streams and fountains. You can create dramatic silhouettes by lighting the wall behind an interesting tree or shrub. Preferably all your fitments should be well hidden behind foliage or boulders; underground well lights which can be hidden behind a grille or toughened safety glass are available from good lighting stockists and specialists.

Lights for use specifically with water features should be waterproof and low voltage; you can buy various types from simple spotlights to elaborate fountain systems that operate in sequence. Most garden lights are available in one of three types: tungsten which produces a warm, yellow light; discharge lighting using sodium or mercury to make a rather blue-green light excellent for highlighting plants and water; and low voltage tungsten halogen lights which have a very white light to display the true natural colour of plants and features and which require a transformer.

A combination of different lighting effects above and on the ground, in and out of the water, produces the most satisfactory, three-dimensional effect. Some lamps are designed to be seen, not hidden away, and lamps and lanterns such as these can look very pretty along a path or lighting up a bridge – a good safety feature too. Alternatively, use underwater lights tucked under the structure. For special occasions, consider garden candles (many of which will repel insects too – an important consideration if you are sitting by a pool or pond), wax flares which you spike into the ground and pretty Chinese lanterns or candles in jam jars to be strung between trees or in trellis and pergola structures.

This series of rocky pools and falls has been spectacularly lit to create a major feature by night as well as during the day.

Wildlife

A pond or pool, however small, will attract a surprising selection of wildlife whether you introduce it or not, especially if it is a natural style and embraces a good variety of plants. Some will arrive courtesy of feeding birds – and you will soon see a greater variety in the garden, maybe even ducks and grebes – others hitch a ride on water plants you may have planted. Many creatures like to breed in or near water so will travel under their own steam. You will soon spot water snails feeding off dead material: the coiled brown ramshorn snail (*Planorbis corneus*) is a useful miniature disposal unit and you may even consider buying three or four of these and introducing them yourself. The great pond snail (*Lymnaea stagnalis*) like a unicorn's horn, is less useful in that it has a taste for ornamental vegetation, especially water-lilies.

There are several familiar insects you will be able to identify straight away if you sit by

the pool and observe it for any length of time: not just the large and lovely dragonfly with its electric colours, but also many shiny blue water boatmen seeming to hover above the water's surface; pond skaters (*Gerris lacustris*) and little water spiders (*Argyroneta aquatis*) spinning their strange silken nests.

Large creatures such as frogs and toads will soon seek out your pool too and you will see the spawn in the water in spring – as soon as the temperature reaches 48–50°F (9–19°C). They are certainly to be encouraged since they eat large numbers of harmful insects and slugs. If you are lucky you may see newts too, but these are becoming increasingly rare.

However, it is the chance to observe fish – maybe even breed them too – that is one of the greatest pleasures of owning a pool. The number of fish you will be able to keep depends on the total surface area of the water – it is better to underestimate the amount of space available. You should aim to have no more than one fish per 2–3sq ft (0.3sq m); Koi carp grow much larger than the average species so they should be calculated at a rate of no more than one fish per 20–25sq ft (2–3sq m). The ubiquitous goldfish (*Carassius auratus*) is easy to keep, grows to a maximum of around 5in (10-12cm) and is an attractive bright gold or silver in colour. Other brightly-coloured fish you might like to consider are the golden rudd (*Scardinious erythrophthalmus*) which is a kind of reddish gold, or the golden orfe (*Idus idus*) for larger pools which grows to an impressive 12in (30cm) and will feed from the surface as well as the bottom. A few scavenger fish like these are useful for keeping the pond clean. Another is the green tench (*Tinca tinca*) although this is rarely seen near the surface.

You will find a wide range of fish at your local water garden centre: darting shubunkins in fluorescent metallic colours or, another hardy fish, the related comets whose colours are not so bright. There are sheeny fantails, veiltails and, of course, Koi carp (*Cyprinus carpio*), those bright and wonderfully patterned fish so strongly associated with the Japanese and their water gardens. They are not difficult to breed but their requirements are quite specific, so you have to be reasonably dedicated to keep them. Many demand high prices – and they need plenty of room, because in ideal conditions they can grow to 3ft (1m). The whole subject is well documented and there are many specialist books on keeping and breeding Koi carp.

Introducing Fish to the Pool

You will not be able to introduce any fish to your pool until it is properly established; that is around two weeks to allow any chlorine in the water to evaporate – remember to use rain-water or tap-water that has

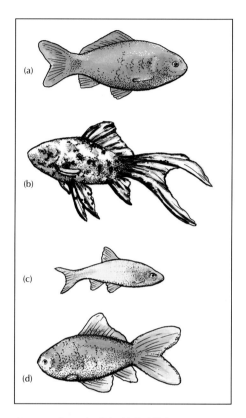

A range of popular fish. (a) Goldfish. (b) Shubunkin. (c) Golden Orfe. (d) Comet.

been allowed to stand and the chlorine evaporated for major top-ups. You could have to wait as long as three months if the pool is lined in concrete, although you can buy proprietary concrete sealants (*see* page 20) if this seems too long. The best time to buy fish for your pool is in the early spring, after the finer days have had a chance to warm the water. Unless the water is particularly warm or chilly, you can just tip the fish straight in. Floating them on top in a plastic bag until the water comes to the same temperature simply puts your fish at risk of suffering from exposure to heat and light.

Few pool owners can resist buying at least a few fish, if only for the pleasure of watching them swimming on lazy afternoons.

A pool or pond might be as small as a single watertight container on the patio with a dwarf lily and a few fish.

Although your fish will find plenty of natural food such as insects in your pool, you may wish to supplement their diet with specially formulated pelleted food during their high activity period in the summer. Fish should only be fed as much as they can eat, so if any food remains, remove it before it decomposes and pollutes the water.

As the weather begins to cool towards winter, the fish's metabolism will slow down and they will require less food. Some types are hardier than others, but none will survive if the pool freezes solid. You can prevent this by investing in a small pond heater which keeps a small area of the pool unfrozen and which is very economical to run. Some owners prefer to overwinter their fish indoors in an aquarium and there are some types which will have to be brought in like any other tender subject. (More pool and water plant wintering techniques are discussed on page 53.)

6 • CARE AND MAINTENANCE

Water features require very little maintenance provided they have been correctly constructed and they are not allowed to get out of hand during the year. It is important, for example, to maintain the correct water level, by topping up in hot weather and draining the excess during periods of heavy rain. This will avoid any erosion of the sides or unnecessary weathering of exposed lining material. Top-ups are preferably made from a rain-water butt provided the water is

clean and not full of leaves or other rotting plant material. During very hot, dry weather you may see your fish coming to the surface and gasping for air; this means oxygen levels have dropped and you will need to drain between one-half and two-thirds of the water and replace with fresh. In drought conditions, turn off any fountains or waterfalls as these lose water through evaporation and replace lost water gradually through a trickling hosepipe rather than letting the water level drop dramatically before refilling. In severe drought, you could try covering the pool with mats to try and reduce evaporation; it would be a good idea in this instance to remove fish to a shaded tank or water butt until conditions have improved.

At the other end of the scale, freezing water can be a problem in winter. Pools deeper than 24in (60cm) are less likely to freeze, particularly if there is a moving water feature such as a fountain or cascade to keep the water circulating. When the pumps and pipes freeze then you do have problems! If you have not transferred your fish to warmer housing, keep an area free

Ligularia przewalskii is another unfussy marginal plant with exciting foliage and flowers. Provided the soil is moist and rich in humus and the plant sheltered from strong winds and sunlight, it produces a large clump of striking dark green, deeply cut leaves and erect spikes of lemon-yellow flowers in mid to late summer. You can propagate new plants by seed in autumn or spring, or by division in spring. The plants tend to be prone to slug and snail damage.

Never try to smash the ice if the water in your pool freezes completely. It is far more efficient – and safer for the fish – to pour a little near-boiling water on to the ice to make a hole. A rubber ball left floating on the water's surface during winter will help to relieve pressure in the event that the water freezes.

from ice with a pool heater. If the pool does freeze over, never try to break the ice by hitting it as the shock waves may stun the fish; thawing a small area with hot water is a far more successful method.

Water health is often a problem, especially with small pools where it can be difficult to achieve the correct biological balance. The result is the all too familiar green scummy pool. This sight simply means long periods of strong sunlight have encouraged algae present in the water to become overprolific and the balance of plants and fish is not sufficient to deal with it. Large pools and ponds fed by moving water do not usually suffer in this way. For a small pool you might try chemical treatment which is supplied in a slow release net which you simply place at the bottom of the pool. Alternatively, you could fit a pool filter which is inexpensive to run yet keeps the water circulating and well aerated – an excellent idea for smaller ponds and pools. There are external types which can be connected to an existing pump and which pass the water through a charcoal filter; and a filter enclosure which is simply a compact

sump in the bottom of the pool with a submersible pump filtering the water through stones and gravel.

If the banks of a pool or stream do become eroded, they must be repaired as soon as possible by driving well-treated timber stakes firmly into the pond or stream

Chipped bark makes a highly attractive pool-edging material, especially in a natural woodland setting. It needs an edging such as stakes or low posts to prevent the material blowing into the water and a good strong marginal plant such as Ligularia clivorum *to bind the bank together.*

bed. You could batten the wood for extra strength and wire this to a chunk of hardwood buried in the ground. The damaged portion of bank can now be backfilled. You can take steps to reduce erosion along shallow, open pond and stream edges: you might insert wooden sleepers backed with shingle; border the banks with boulders and smaller stones; or line the edge of the pool with paving slabs.

Linings can be repaired if they suffer damage, but the pool or pond will have to be drained – a good excuse for a clear-out perhaps. If you are working on a plastic or butyl-lined pool, do be careful that your boots do not rip the bottom or sides of the

Green water can be a problem, especially in small pools where it may be difficult to maintain a good biological balance.

pool further when you attempt your repair. You must make sure that the area to be repaired is completely dry and clean, then prepare a butyl or bitumen plastic patch big enough to cover the tear. Make sure you know exactly which material your particular pool is made of so that you can buy a patch to match. Both surfaces must be free from grease or dirt; rubbing with talcum cleaner helps key the surface. First brush the torn liner with a suitable waterproof latex solution then apply it to the patch, making sure the whole surface is covered. As soon as the glue reaches the recommended 'tacky' stage, press the patch firmly into position making sure there are no air pockets. You must then paint over the whole area with the adhesive and wait at least six hours before refilling the pool to make sure it is dry.

Autumn and winter are not good times to clean out or repair a pond or pool because you will disturb plants and fish already acclimatizing themselves to the changing temperatures. Spring is a much better time when fish are feeding regularly and plants are growing vigorously, which will help them recover quickly from any shock.

Concrete ponds can usually be repaired by forcing fresh concrete into the cracks after draining the pool. It is a good idea to cover the new areas with sealant to ensure they are watertight and to reduce the risk of any toxins leaching out into the water. Preformed fibreglass pools can be repaired using a fibreglass repair kit; these can be found in chandlers or other boat repair stockists.

Generally, a water feature requires very little attention during the almost dormant months of winter. The only chore might be keeping the water free from leaves. These settle on the bottom of the pond or pool and begin to decay causing unwelcome gases which will eventually cause the water to go black and stagnant. Small pools can be netted as soon as the leaves start to fall.

Alternatively, you could fish the leaves out regularly with a soft plastic scoop or rake. Any rotting vegetation should be removed carefully and marginal plants tidied up after the first frosts. This is also a good time to rake out excess, dead or diseased floating weed. This is not generally so much of a problem if the pool is fed by running water. With large pools and lakes, excessive weed and plant growth is usually removed with a special fork-like tool called a chrome which is used to twist it out like spaghetti.

Moving Water Features

A moving water feature can be kept running all winter if you wish and, since running water does not freeze as easily as still water, this can be a useful way to keep the water from freezing. Running on very cold nights is advisable to prevent the water pipes from freezing. During extended freezing periods, you may prefer to remove the feature altogether, clean it, dry it and store it in the shed or garage. You should keep the pipes free from dirt and debris all year round and the pipework may have to be treated at regular intervals if you live in a hard water area to prevent narrow valves and nozzles being clogged up with lime.

Pumps actually run better if you leave them going all the time, even overnight, as the surge of water when the pump is turned on and off can clog the filter. Surface pumps must be provided with a waterproof shelter and all moving parts ought to be kept well greased and oiled to prevent them from seizing up. It is important that a surface pump is not run dry or that you do not forget to release the valve that allows water from the pond to reach the pump. Most models have a bleed screw that ensures there is water in the chamber before the pump is turned on. They should be drained, turned off and overhauled in winter. Submersible pumps are generally made from plastic and are self-lubricating so require minimum maintenance. They should be stripped down and serviced annually by a reputable dealer. In dirty water or a pond with lots of plants, it would be worth cleaning the filter every week. The pump can be hauled to the surface for this job.

Pool Surrounds

The areas surrounding a pool or water feature

This free-standing water feature cleverly combines the charms of a pool with built-in seating for observing fish and water plants within a structure reminiscent of an old wishing well. With weathered timber giving an instantly mellow feel, this is a feature which could be incorporated anywhere in the garden.

should be checked regularly to make sure they are safe and are in good condition. Pavers, bricks and tiles require very little maintenance other than sweeping clear of leaves and any occasional oily marks removed using a proprietary patio cleaner. Any pointing that has been damaged by frost should be raked out and replaced before the problem worsens and the surface material works loose. Exposed timbers will need treating with preservative once a year and any wooden surfaces underfoot scoured with a wire brush to remove slippery lichen growth. It is worth also keeping an eye out for any rusting or missing screws and nails. Handrails will also require regular attention to ensure they are safe.

Plants

Water plants could not be easier to look after; apart from slug damage (a healthy population of frogs or toads is your best environment-friendly answer here) their main problem is that they grow too rampantly. To prevent one species taking hold and swamping the others to spoil your display, plants should be thinned, divided or cut back in autumn. Spraying the leaves regularly with fresh water during warm weather helps to knock any insects off the leaves into the water where they will be eaten by fish. Water-lilies can sometimes be attacked by the lily beetle and these are best picked off and crushed; they are also prone to aphids which can be wiped off the leaves with damp cotton wadding. It is better not to use chemical treatments if you can because these not only pollute the water, they can be harmful to other wildlife too.

Some plants grow a little too vigorously and may threaten to take over the whole feature. Most water species tend to be a little rampant and regular cutting back usually keeps them under control.

However, some of the weeds can be a real menace. Blanketweed can quickly cover the whole surface in green and because it is filamentous it is a nuisance to remove. The easiest method is to take a strong piece of wood and to twist it in the weed, rotating it round the pool at the same time. The threads of weed should attach themselves to the wood. Duckweed can also be a problem as it multiplies quickly; this floating plant is best removed by dragging the surface of the pond with an old butterfly net.

Fish

Fish are usually relatively problem-free but if you do notice one of the following symptoms, act immediately.

If the fish is seen floating on its back, transfer to an aquarium of salt-water in a ratio of a teaspoonful per gallon (4.5 litres) to revive it.

If your fish keep coming to the surface and gulping air, there is too little oxygen in the water. The temperature may be too high or you may have too many fish in the pool. Oxygenate the water by replacing around a third to two-thirds of the water or by turning on a waterfall or fountain if you have one. Alternatively, remove the fish and transfer them to a large tank or bath of water; if the problem recurs you will have to reduce their numbers.

Any strange bumps, lumps, patches or white cotton-like growths that appear on the fish should be noted, and these fish separated from the healthy stock. Your local fish stockist will be able to recommend a proprietary treatment.

Propagation of Plants

Water and moisture-loving plants are usually propagated by taking cuttings or by division of the crowns or rhizomes, particularly since they are so prolific and will probably require thinning or splitting at the end of the growing year in any case. Seeds can be gathered when ripe and stored in a dry place until the following spring which minimizes common problems with seedlings damping off. Sow in spring in small flowerpots filled with seed compost; mixing the seeds with sand or planting gel helps to ensure a more even distribution of very fine seeds. The pots are then placed in an aquarium two-thirds full of water until the seedlings are large enough to handle, at which point they are replanted in pots of growing compost. These are replaced in the aquarium until large enough and sturdy enough to be replanted in their final positions once there is no more risk of frost. If there is a danger of bird damage, use netting over them during the day.

Any water plants with elongated axil joints can be propagated easily by taking

Planting seeds: simply cover with a fine layer of sand.

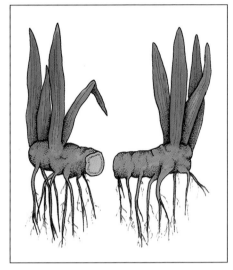

Dividing a rhizome: cut with a sharp knife, making sure that there are no snags or jagged edges that will allow disease to enter.

Taking a cutting: remove the base leaves, leaving only one or two.

cuttings. These are taken using a sharp knife at the axil joints where the secondary buds form, and any leaves removed. The cuttings should be no longer than 2in (5cm) long. Warmth and plenty of daylight are essential for their growth, so the best time to take cuttings is as early as possible in spring or summer. The cuttings can be positioned around the edge of a flowerpot filled with one-part peat, one-part well-rotted cow manure and one-part sharp sand. The pot can now be placed in a shallow part of the pond until the cuttings have rooted and can be transferred to their permanent positions. This is best delayed until they are quite large as they are not deep-rooted species. You may be lucky enough to get a good crop of self-sets – that is, new plants which have shooted a little distance from the parent plant. These can be carefully removed and used as new young stock,

perhaps to be sold or exchanged with friends or family for different species.

Water plants can also be propagated by division. Plants with crowns have compacted leaf axil joints and they are more easily propagated by crown division. The plant is gently lifted, and using two forks back-to-back at its centre the crown can be divided in two by carefully pulling the two forks apart. The divisions should be placed in a pot of John Innes No 2 until they have established roots, then they can be transplanted to their permanent positions. Water-lilies can also be divided. These are rhizomatous plants: you must lift them in spring and cut the rhizome into pieces about 4in (10cm) long with a sharp knife. You can plant the pieces in the pool in the same way as you would the main plant. If the root has several eyes reduce these to no more than three, as the weaker buds will only reduce the success of the main shoots.

7 • SEASON BY SEASON GUIDE

Spring

● At the first hint of warmer weather the pond or pool comes to life, set to become a major feature of garden or patio until the first frosts wither flowers and foliage. The brilliant gold flowers of the marsh marigolds are usually the first to appear, making a wonderfully fresh display against the light green of the fleshy leaves. With plants and wildlife coming to life again, now is the best time to carry out any necessary repairs or proposed changes – when everything will have plenty of time to recuperate.

● You will notice much increased activity amongst your pool fish. They will not be in peak condition having lain low all winter, so look out for any signs of disease such as fungal infections and treat accordingly. Start feeding a little supplementary food, increasing the amount daily as they begin to take it until you find the limit they will consume. Generally fish will start to feed as soon as the water reaches a certain temperature.

● Look out for spawn in the water – a sign that local frogs or toads have discovered your pool. You may well hear them croaking mournfully in the evenings. If you would like frogs in your garden but they do not visit, ask around for spawn (local conservation groups are a good source) as now is the time to introduce it. You must not remove spawn from ponds in the wild.

● If the water has become polluted with decaying vegetation or the pool liner has been damaged by severe winter weather, now is the best time to drain or partially drain the water. You should first remove any dead or decaying material and then pump out (or use buckets) about a third of the total volume of water for a water change – or probably all of it for a repair. You should always take water from the top of the pool so as not to upset the natural biological balance. You can top it up again with tap-water, but since this usually contains chlorine and other chemicals it is better, if you can, to use rain-water from a butt. Always add it via a hosepipe set at a slow trickle. You will have to remove any fish and other wildlife to an aquarium if emptying the pool, otherwise they should not come to harm remaining in the pool.

● The worst frosts should be over now so start tidying up marginal and bog plants around the pool. Any remains of last year's growth should be removed and plants generally tidied up, taking care dead vegetation does not drop into the water.

● Provided there is no longer any risk of the kind of cold weather that will freeze your pond solid, remove the pond heater, clean it and pack it away.

Hosta is prized mainly for its foliage which is thick, fleshy and deeply veined – a wonderful contrast to taller, spikier plants. Growing in a dense clump and enjoying moist conditions, it makes good ground cover right to the water's edge, without being too invasive like other pool-edge and bog garden plants. They do prefer a shadier position but some will tolerate full sun if conditions are damp enough. The flowers are something of a bonus and are attractive: usually violet or mauve, they are held above the foliage on long stems. There are various forms and colours including striped and flecked foliage. This is *Hosta fortunei* 'Aurea Marginata' which has golden yellow edges and is one of the first to appear in spring. Hosta is prone to slug and snail damage.

● Spring is the best time to germinate seeds of many interesting bog garden species so plant these now.

● As the days lengthen, plants will be growing vigorously; water plants do not produce hardwood so late spring is a good time to plant new varieties.

● This is also a good time to take a long look at all your existing plants and take out or transplant where necessary to stop them being too invasive. This will still give replanted specimens a chance to recuperate and make up good growth.

● Remove and thin out overcrowded water-lilies that have not been performing so well lately. Provided there are plenty of new buds growing from the roots, they should do well. You can buy a special pond

fertilizer pellet where soluble nutrient is enclosed in clay to keep it at the bottom of the pool. You should never use general purpose fertilizers in a pool as they cloud the water.

Summer

● When there is no danger whatsoever of any more frosts, you can plant out your tropical water-lilies, water chestnuts and water hyacinth.

● With the warmer weather comes the problem of insects. It is best to use chemicals as little as possible in or around water as they can build up to toxic levels as well as kill off natural predators and alter the

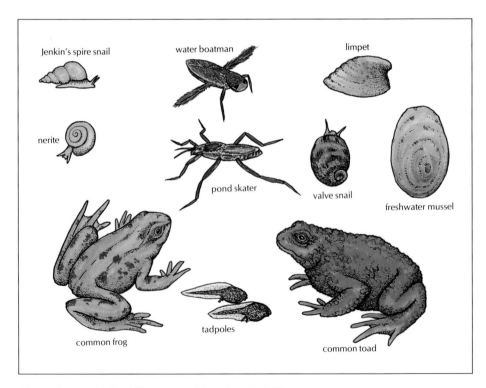

The smallest pond will quickly attract a wide variety of wildlife.

water's natural ecological balance. It is better to try and spot any kind of infestation as early as possible and to remove any infected foliage immediately. Aphids may be washed off foliage with a firm jet of water and they will be eaten by your fish.

● Look out for any fish eggs and remove them to a fish-free pond or an aquarium.

● During hot weather when the water will be getting warmer and the levels of oxygen dropping, use a small air pump or turn on a moving water feature, such as a fountain or waterfall if you have one, to generate a little extra oxygen for wildlife in the water.

● Water the bog garden carefully during dry weather (*see* page 53).

● Collect seed from any early flowering species which have now finished.

● Keep vigorous marginal and aquatic plants cut back and under control through-out the season. One species could quickly and easily dominate if given its head.

● Remove spreading blanketweed immediately you see it growing, using a stout piece of wood, before it takes over the whole water's surface.

● Continue to keep a close watch for any aphid infection and treat immediately as recommended before.

Autumn

● As the days shorten and temperatures drop, plants will begin to die back although in the well planned water garden there will still be something of interest to carry you through to the first frosts. Remove any dead or decaying material and cut back rampant pond weeds again as soon as they look like becoming a problem.

● Move tender plants such as water hyacinths, tropical lilies and water chestnuts plus any tender fish into an indoor aquarium in a warm greenhouse.

● Place the pond heater in position and switch on at the earliest frost warnings or hint of a fine clear sky. If you have no heater, a plastic ball on the water's surface will help prevent it freezing over.

● When giant *Gunnera manicata* has died down, the leaves are usually folded over the crown for winter protection.

● Net the pool if falling leaves are a pollution problem.

Winter

● Plants and grass still grow – if slowly – during the colder winter months. Keep the water garden and surrounding areas looking tidy by removing any dead material as required and mowing grass on the highest setting of the machine.

● Fish will stop taking food as the weather becomes cooler so you can cease feeding them until next spring.

● Take care that the pond does not freeze over totally; poisonous gases build up and cannot escape through the ice so will poison fish. Make a hole using a kettle of hot water. Never try to crack open the ice using a bar as this will probably stun your fish and the water immediately refreezes in any case.

● Check all relevant equipment, such as pumps, hoses and jets, and have them serviced if necessary.

● Inspect the pool or pond regularly to make sure there has been no sudden drop in the water levels as this will mean a leak and necessary repairs.

● Since marginal and bog plants are expensive, why not try and grow a few yourself? Small plants might be sold or exchanged in summer for varieties you do not have.

GLOSSARY

Algae Simple organisms which thrive in light warm conditions and cause pond-water to look bright green where its natural ecological balance may have broken down.

Annual Plant which completes its life cycle and dies within a period of a year.

Aquatic Plant capable of living with its roots, stems and sometimes leaves submerged in water.

Backfilling Adding soil, hardcore and so on to bring an area to the desired level.

Ball valve Automatic device used to control the water level of a pool. The lightweight ball floats on the surface of the water and when the water level drops, a rod attached to the ball releases a valve which allows water to flow in. As the ball rises, the rod gradually closes the valve.

Bearers Load-bearing timbers used in the construction of timber decks, pergolas etc.

Bevelled A sloped edge – on timber, for example, where it gives a neat finish.

Biennial Plant that completes its life cycle within two years.

Bobcat Small earth-moving machine useful for excavating small ponds.

Bog Damp area of rich, poorly-drained soil that remains waterlogged under normal conditions. Sometimes developed as a bog garden using the kind of plants normally found near streams and pools.

Bubble fountain Low bubbling fountain effect created using a pump concealed in an underground reservoir of water.

Bulb A storage organ or swollen leaf base containing the necessary food for a resting period.

Butyl Waterproof rubber material used to line pools and other water features.

Calcareous Soil containing chalk or lime.

Chlorine Chemical used to sterilize water.

Clay Heavy sticky soil type containing fine sand and alumina.

Clay puddling Technique used to seal and waterproof the sides and base of large natural ponds using hand, foot or machine to knead clay to a watertight finish.

Conduit A channel or pipe used as a protective cover, usually for electric cables.

Corm Storage organ in the form of a swollen underground stem.

Crown Top of the rootstock from which new shoots grow.

Cultivar Cultivated variety incapable of exact reproduction from seed. May be naturally occurring or artificially created.

Culvert Channel or conduit for carrying water, electric cables and so on. A large concrete culvert could be used as the basis for an arched bridge.

Decking Timber platform structure supported by bearers and used to create a patio or jetty area.

Dormancy Period of inactivity usually induced when temperatures drop.

Dumper-mounted back-hoe Small earth-moving machine useful in the excavation of ponds and pools.

Erosion Wearing away and destruction of soil, rock and so on due to the effects of wind and rain.

Exotic Plant not indigenous to the country in which it is growing and where it cannot naturalize.

Filter Device used for removing suspended particles of organic matter from the water.

Friable Soil that crumbles easily due to high organic content.

Fungicide Substance – usually containing copper or sulphur – which is used to destroy fungal disease.

Genus Term used to identify a family of plants.

Gravel Mixture of rock fragments and small pebbles.

Half hardy Plant that requires protection from frost in winter.

Hardcore Rough stones, brick or pebbles used to create a firm base for concreting, sometimes called ballast.

Hardwood Resilient timber from deciduous trees.

Herbaceous Plant producing only soft sappy growth instead of wood.

Hot tub Large wooden barrel fitted with seats and connected to a pump, filter, heater and bubble equipment.

Humus Decayed organic matter used as a rich soil conditioner.

Hybrid Cross between plants of different species.

Inorganic Fertilizer or any chemical compound without carbon.

Insecticide Chemical developed to kill insects.

JCB Large earth-moving machine for excavation of larger pools.

Joists Parallel timbers used to support boards such as timber decking.

Landscaping Garden design in imitation of the natural landscape. Also integrating a new feature into an existing design.

Loam Rotted turf, usually in a mixture of sand, clay and humus.

Marginal Plant which grows in the shallows of a pool or stream or in waterlogged soil.

Marginal shelf Shallow shelf built into the side of a pool where marginal plants can be planted or stood in special baskets.

Masonry bolt Expanding rawlbolt for extremely strong fixing of timber, usually into stone or brickwork.

Mini Hymac Small earth-moving machine used in the excavation of pools and ponds.

Mulch Decayed or part-decayed organic material spread around the base of plants to reduce evaporation of moisture from the soil and to suppress weeds.

Naturalize Growing plants under conditions that are as natural as possible. Plants that were originally imported but which have reseeded themselves in the wild are known as naturalized.

Nursery bed Separate soil bed reserved for seeding and growing young plants until large enough to be planted out.

Oxygenating Describes a plant that grows in or under water and which produces oxygen.

Perennial Plant that lives and flowers for a number of years.

Pergola Trellis structure made of timber, metal or brick used to create arbours, arches and walkways covered in climbing plants.

Photosynthesis Process used by plants where energy is absorbed by chlorophyll from sunlight.

Pier Column support for a bridge or arch.

Propagation Producing new plants by seeding, layering, cutting, division or grafting.

Pump Device for raising or moving water.

RCCB Residual current circuit breaker – a cut-out safety device which is triggered by any irregularity in the electric current.

Rhizome Underground stem that grows horizontally and puts up stems some distance from the parent plant.

Shingle Small round pebbles sometimes used as a surface material.

Shuttering Timber used to construct a temporary support for wet concrete.

Softwood Soft timber from conifers.

Species Group of plants alike in appearance, breed and character.

Spirit-level Device used to check the horizontal or vertical planes of a construction.

Stagnant Water that is stale and sluggish.

Straight-edge Piece of straight, unwarped timber used to maintain a straight line.

Subsoil Layer of poor, organically-deficient soil found beneath the surface.

Tap root Straight, often central, root, from which subsidiary roots grow.

Topsoil Top layer of soil usually comprising good organic matter.

T-piece T-shaped connection used to join three different pipes.

Variegated Leaves with variety of coloured markings: silver, gold, blue, grey, white on green, white, bronze and so on.

Watercourse Formal waterway usually with straight parallel sides.

Water table Level under the ground to which water naturally drains.

Weir Dam built across a stream or river and designed to raise the water level upstream.

Well light Outdoor lighting fitment which can be hidden underground and covered with specially toughened glass safety lens.

INDEX